HERSHEY GARDENS

The Cornfield that Blossomed with Roses

---

by Mary Davidoff Houts

This publication was made possible by grants from:

Pennsylvania Historical and Museum Commission

Conard-Pyle Roses

Brownstone Real Estate, Country Market Nursery, Dutch Mill Bulbs,
Dr. and Mrs. Benjamin Paul Ebersole, Hershey Entertainment and Resorts,
Hershey Gardens Staff Gardeners and Dr. and Mrs. Dennis Johnson

Design by Joe Roman of Schreiber & Roman, Inc., Elizabethtown, PA
Printed in the United States of America by Innovative Technologies in Print, Elizabethtown, PA

Visit Hershey Gardens on the internet at http://www.hersheygardens.org

Acknowledgements

The author is indebted to the many people who assisted in the development of this book. First and foremost is Peter Houts who not only took the majority of the modern-day photographs but also provided encouragement and counsel throughout. Special credit is also due to Barbara Whitcraft, Hershey Gardens Director of Horticulture, whose work in the gardens has been a continuing source of inspiration and who was a patient provider of Gardens information. The author also owes appreciation to the Hershey Gardens staff gardeners and Grounds Manager Jamie Shiffer who were supportive and accommodating at all times.

Many thanks for continuing advice and support from Marta Howell, Executive Director of the M.S. Hershey Foundation and from the Hershey Gardens Advisory Board, especially the Book Committee consisting of Donna Evans, Director of Development, M.S. Hershey Foundation; Trish Foulkrod; Craig George, Hershey Gardens Director; Jan Hester, Hershey Gardens Retail Operations Manager; Karen Johnson, Advisory Board President; Janet Maynard, Advisory Board Secretary; Lynn Neeley; Jill Manley, Director of Marketing and Public Relations, The M.S. Hershey Foundation; Ashie Santangelo and Barbara Whitcraft. Thanks also to Cherylann Wagner of Flowers Designs by Cherylann, Ltd. for her contribution towards publication.

Research for the historical section of the book was mainly conducted at the Hershey Community Archives where Pamela Whitenack, Director and Archivist, and staff members Diane Summers and Judy Grow were unfailingly helpful. The majority of the early historical pictures are from this Archives. Amy Bischof, Senior Curator, Hershey Museum; Millie Landis-Coyle, Hershey-Derry Township Historical Society; Michael Sherbon, Pennsylvania State Archives; Neil Fasnacht, Barbara Whitcraft and Rachel Wolgemuth were also generous in sharing their knowledge of pertinent history and sources of historic photographs. Marlin Buck, Neil Fasnacht, Ellis Kreider, Carol Humphreys, Judy White and Richard Williams permitted the use of pictures from their personal collections. Michael P. Dineen, Publisher and Editorial Director and owner of the film and rights to the book, *Great Gardens of America* published by Country Beautiful Foundation, gave permission to take a photograph of the book cover in the Hershey Community Archives collection for use in this publication. The search for photographs from recent times was aided by Jill Manley and Barbara Whitcraft and by former Gardens Public Relations Directors Susan Klein and Amy Taber. Janet Maynard and Michael Seligson of the Hershey Camera Club and Richard A. Walter generously contributed pictures that they took in the Gardens over the past year.

Credits for specific photographs may be found on Page 88.

The following people who were or still are directly involved with the Gardens graciously granted one-on-one interviews to the author: Albert Bos (retired), Dutch Mill Bulbs; Bill Bowman and Mark Gruin, former Gardens Directors; David L. Parke, Jr., former Gardens Executive Director; Leone Gerberich and Crystal Huff, formerly of the Gardens Staff; Ruth Holp and Dr. Benjamin P. Ebersole, both lifetime neighbors of the Gardens and current Gardens staff Barbara Whitcraft and Jamie Shiffer.

The author is also grateful to those who read and commented on all or portions of the manuscript: Eliza Harrison, former Director of the Hershey Museum; Kenneth Hatt, President and COO (retired) and John Zerbe, President and COO (retired), Hershey Entertainment and Resorts Company; Marta Howell; Elizabeth Lewis, Manhattanville College; Pamela Whitenack and present and former Gardens staff, Barbara Whitcraft, Jamie Shiffer, Mark Gruin, Leone Gerberich and Hershey Gardens Staff Gardeners. The work of Dr. Judith T. Witmer as copy editor is greatly appreciated.

Responsibility for the final text, including any factual errors or omissions, rests with the author.

Mary D. Houts
Hummelstown, PA
May, 2006

CONTENTS

Hershey Gardens
INTRODUCTION

Up on a hill
north of
Hershey,
Pennsylvania
there is a
garden
filled with
color and
lovely vistas.

In the garden there are *sweeping views*

and *small, quiet places.*

Unusual
trees and
striking
flower beds
provide
interest
and
beauty.

A captivating

*children's
garden*

and
a fascinating
butterfly
house
add life and
activity.

Tourists love the garden, but it's a great place for the **community** too.

It's a spectacular place for *weddings*.

The garden has become a Hershe

People who enjoyed it as *children*

brought *their* childre

There are *classes* for children and adults and many kinds of *events* are held on the grounds.

radition since it opened in 1937.

and now bring their *grandchildren* to enjoy the garden...

winter

spring

ll year round

summer

and *fall*.

View to the South from Hershey Gardens, 2000's. (Hersheypark rides and the original Hershey chocolate factory can be seen in the distance.) The factory, amusement park and garden are all part of the legacy of Milton Hershey. He created them between 1903 and 1937 as components of his model town. The History of the Gardens section of this book shows how the creation of the garden was a natural outcome of Mr. Hershey's vision for his town and how the garden has survived and flourished through changing and often challenging times.

HISTORY OF THE GARDENS

"The more beautiful you can make the place look,

the better life people will have."

– Milton S. Hershey

ONE

A Tradition of Landscaping and Public Gardens

Long before Hershey Gardens first opened in 1937 as the Hershey Rose Garden, the town of Hershey had a history of fine landscaping and public gardens. Right from the start of their planned community in 1903, Milton and Catherine Hershey believed that greenery and gardens should be a priority. Residential lots were made large enough so that home buyers could have lawns and gardens. Mr. Hershey hired a landscape architect from Philadelphia to draw up landscaping plans for the public sections of the town. He also hired a chief gardener and provided him with staff to plant and maintain the street trees and public gardens called for in the plans.

Tourists and townspeople alike enjoyed visiting Hershey's landscaped public areas. The gardens surrounding the chocolate factory, the green and flowery amusement park and displays in the town greenhouses all could be visited without charge. Even the grounds of the Hersheys' own home, including its large greenhouse, were open to the public.

Visitors could also enjoy the large naturalistic park located on the hill north of town where Hotel Hershey now stands. Trails and roads were built through it so that people could drive, walk or take a trolley to enjoy the landscaping and the expansive view from the top. The hill's south side, however, where Hershey Gardens is located today, was used for farming.

High Point Mansion Grounds, 1913. The public was welcome to visit the strikingly landscaped grounds of the Hershey mansion which overlooked the chocolate factory.

History of the Gardens

Oglesby Paul, ca. 1910. Mr. Paul, the head landscape gardener at Philadelphia's Fairmount Park, was hired by the Hersheys to draw up landscaping plans for their mansion and the town.

Pond on High Point Mansion Grounds, ca. 1909 – 1918. Trees in tubs, like those seen here, were overwintered in Hershey greenhouses and brought out to enhance landscaping around town.

West End of Hershey Chocolate Company Factory and Office, (Pennsylvania and Reading Railroad Passenger Station is at the left) ca. 1915. The railroad put large flower beds around the station so that their landscaping would compare favorably to that of the adjoining factory.

Hershey Park, ca. 1915. In the early days, before there were many rides, the park had large landscaped areas where people could spend time relaxing. This was an especially important reason for visiting the park.

Hershey Park (now Hersheypark®) Entrance, ca. 1920 – 1929. One of the reasons that Hershey Park has appealed to visitors since its founding in 1907 is its attractive landscaping.

Chocolate Avenue, ca. 1914 – 1918. As the town grew, the streets were lined with trees. By 1917, many thousands of tree as well as flowering plants and shrubs, had been planted in th town and on Milton Hershey's extensive properties in the area

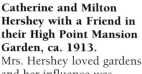

Catherine and Milton Hershey with a Friend in their High Point Mansion Garden, ca. 1913.
Mrs. Hershey loved gardens and her influence was prevalent in the amount and kinds of landscaping in the town.

Hershey Mansion Greenhouse, ca. 1916. Large displays of carnations, lilies, geraniums, tropicals and other plants could be enjoyed here by the public.

Harry Haverstick, Hershey's First Chief Gardener, 1917. Milton Hershey hired Haverstick in 1905 to be in charge of carrying out the landscaping and grounds maintenance in the town and on all of the Hershey properties. A chief gardener with a horticultural staff were kept on the payroll throughout Mr. Hershey's lifetime.

NOW IS THE TIME TO GET BUSY

Plan and Plant Should be the Duties of These Days That Look Towards the Spring. The Idea is to Make Hershey the Real Floral Town. Helps.

Plant more flowers this year.
The Hershey idea will not be complete until there are flowers in front of every house in the town. This is not a complaint of the past, for during the past few years there has been great progress. Especially last year the showing was excellent. There were twice as many flowers in the yards and gardens of Hershey last year than there were two years previous.

But better can be done and now is the time to begin.
It makes no difference how narrow may be your house or yard front you can make it more attractive by vines and flowers. There is special need of better treatment of the ground walls of houses, all of which should be lined with vines or flowers. -If your front yard is only a small plot see that it has a rose bush or two this year.

Last year the bulk of the flowers were in the rear and many of them were missed by the public because they could not be seen from the main avenues. Put out more of your bulbs and plants in front. Your flowers are not only pleasures for your own family but are contributions to the general good. People like to see flowers in front of houses. In fact a home without flowers does not seem a home—only a building. Possibly you have room for only a vase. Then put it up. It need not be an expensive one. Just a home-made thing will do, and when it is covered with vines and blooms it will have richness that money could not buy.

There must be more window boxes in Hershey. Fine things were done last year, but there is a demand for more. Now is the time to get busy on your window boxes.

Spring Flower Show, Hershey Zoo Greenhouse, ca. 1916.
From 1911–1917, an elaborate flower show with masses of spring bulbs and other flowering plants was held each year in all three of the town's greenhouses. On Easter Sunday in 1917, 5,000 people came to see the display.

Article from *The Hershey Press*, February 1, 1917.
The newspaper, run by the Hershey interests from 1909 to 1926, periodically reminded townsfolk how important the landscaping around their homes was to the image of the town.

Cocoa Avenue Residences, ca. 1920.
Mr. Hershey made sure that building lots were large enough so that residents would have room for lawns and gardens.

TWO

The Early Years: 1936 – 1945

In response to the Great Depression in the early 1930's, Milton Hershey began a local building campaign as a way to provide employment for jobless citizens of the area. He had many public buildings erected and in 1936 work was started on the Hershey Rose Garden.

Horace McFarland, a Harrisburger nationally known for his work in civic beautification and in the American Rose Society, convinced Mr. Hershey that he should build a public rose garden. The idea fit in well with a plan that he had already been contemplating for the development of a public garden south of the new Hotel Hershey, so he decided to go ahead and have a 3.5 acre Hershey Rose Garden built there. During the summer and fall of 1936 the site was prepared, beds were laid out and 12,500 rose bushes of 112 varieties were planted. From the time it opened in June 1937, the Hershey Rose Garden was an instant and continuing success with the public.

Delighted by the popularity of the garden, Milton Hershey had new rose beds added each year. In 1941, the addition of adjoining farm fields brought it to its present size of 23 acres. Just before World War II, the new acreage was contoured and planted with annuals, perennials, tulips and other bulbs, specimen trees and flowering shrubs. Until the time of his death in 1945, Mr. Hershey visited the Rose Garden often. He got great pleasure from the peace and beauty he found there and from watching the visitors enjoying it as well.

Opening Day at Hershey Rose Garden, June 2, 1937.
Right from the start, people poured in by the thousands to see this beautifully situated free attraction with its astonishing mass of bloom.

J. Horace McFarland, Environmentalist and Rose Expert, 1947. He suggested that Milton Hershey either make a public rose garden in the Hershey area or donate a million dollars for a national rosarium near Washington, D.C. Mr. Hershey chose to build the Hershey Rose Garden.

Hershey Rose Garden Construction Site, Summer 1936. Work continued throughout the summer. By early November, all of the 12,500 rose bushes were in the ground. They were so well planted that all but eleven survived the winter.

Design for the Hershey Rose Garden, 1936. Hershey's chief gardener, Harry Erdman, designed a first-class rose garden about the size of three and a half football fields.

Harry Erdman with Two Garden Visitors, ca. 1950's. Erdman had been in charge of horticulture for Hershey since the late 1920's. Although he had no special knowledge of roses before creating the Hershey Rose Garden, he soon became a nationally respected expert.

Milton Hershey and Harry Erdman Inspecting the Reflecting Pond at the Rose Garden Site, August 1936. Hershey liked the fact that the site was within walking distance for Hotel Hershey guests. Erdman said one of the best things about the site was that "the magnificent erosion gully that resulted from the construction of the hotel… made a wonderful pond for irrigation and ornamentation."

Hershey Rose Garden, June 1937. "Harry L. Erdman deserves great credit for his success in having achieved within a few short months a surpassing abundance of uniformly luxuriant blooms," said *Success with Roses* magazine.

View Looking North from the Reflecting Pond, Summer 1938. The pond was a much admired feature of the garden. Reflections of the many roses added to the brilliance of the scene and the imposing Hotel Hershey's reflection also appeared in the pond at certain times of day.

Official Dedication of the Hershey Rose Garden, September 5, 1938. The ceremony, which took place during the 40th annual meeting of the American Rose Society, was held on the porch of the brand new sales building.

Rose Garden Third Unit, October 15, 1938. After only two years the Garden had been enlarged to 6.5 acres and the number of rose bushes increased to approximately 25,000. *Horticulture Magazine* labeled it as "one of the world's notable rose gardens."

The 'M.S. Hershey' Rose, 1941. A commercial grower named this rose in recognition of what Milton Hershey's Rose Garden had done to heighten interest in roses. Red roses were among Mr. Hershey's favorite flowers.

Rose Named For M. S. Hershey

Hershey, Pa.,—In honor of M. S. Hershey's 83rd birthday, the American Rose Society named a new rose for the philanthropist. It is a hybrid tea seedling with a long, pointed bud, double-flowered, high centered, slightly fragrant, and velvety crimson-red in color.

The naming of the new rose came about through Mr. Hershey's interest in roses. In 1936 he created a rose garden, free to the public, which has increased from 12,500 rose plants at its beginning to almost double that number now, with varieties numbering over 700.

The dedication of the rose garden by the American Rose Society in the Fall of 1938 was followed by a dinner here at which Mary N. Dixon, of Farmingdale, Long Island, read a poem in which she urged that M. S. Hershey's name should be given to one of the new roses.

L. B. Codington, of Summit, N. J., who originated the rose President Hoover, was present and at that time was experimenting upon a new hybrid tea seedling for which he later obtained a patent; the name acceptable to the American Rose Society.

Two stanzas of the Dixon poem follow:

To illustrate just what we mean:
  Here's one for which we'd all be keen
'Twould lend a Rose enduring fame
How's M. S. Hershey for a name!

And in our gardens, you can bet,
  We'd surely keep his feet well wet
For Mr. Hershey is a king
And rates the best of everything.

World War II Soldier at Hershey Rose Garden, Early 1940's. An outing to the garden was a welcome escape from war-time stresses. Unfortunately, gasoline rationing made a visit there a rare luxury and caused visitation to drop to 10 percent of pre-war numbers.

Aerial View, Expanded Rose Garden, ca. 1941-1950. When Mr. Hershey added 17 acres of farmland to the Rose Garden in 1941, he allowed Harry Erdman to spend what was necessary to landscape it with many different kinds of plants. Erdman's long term goal was to include every kind of woody and herbaceous plant that would grow in Pennsylvania.

Great Gardens
of America

General Editor
Carroll C. Calkins

THREE

The Postwar Years: 1946 – 1969

As the country settled back into a peacetime mode after World War II, Hershey once again became a mecca for an ever-increasing number of tourists. The Rose Garden continued to be one of the town's major attractions, and the Hershey interests made sure that its strong points were used to help bring the town to the attention of the public. A featured event for the town's 50th anniversary, in 1953, was a statewide contest for a Hershey Garden Rose Queen. Throughout the 1950's and 1960's festivals were held to highlight the garden during its peak blooming seasons.

Many beautiful and interesting collections of different kinds of plants were added in the postwar years. These included woody plants such as weeping trees, dwarf conifers, boxwoods, and Japanese maples as well as daylilies, chrysanthemums and other herbaceous species. It was still the roses, however, that gave the garden its unique identity. It had one of the largest rose displays anywhere in the country and maintained an excellent horticultural reputation.

However, by the end of the 1960's, financial support was becoming a problem. Milton Hershey had wanted the garden as a jewel in the crown of his green and landscaped town, and during his lifetime he saw to it that the Rose Garden was well funded. Those who followed Mr. Hershey sought to retain this legacy, but he had left no endowment for the garden and they were finding it increasingly difficult to pay the bills.

***Great Gardens of America*, 1969.** The Hershey Rose Garden's postwar reputation as a public garden worthy of national attention was reinforced when it was not only included in this book, but also featured on the cover.

Colorama Queen, 1969. During the postwar years the garden became a focal point for a variety of public events. Fall Colorama was a festival featuring the chrysanthemum display. There were rose and tulip festivals as well.

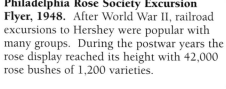

Philadelphia Rose Society Excursion Flyer, 1948. After World War II, railroad excursions to Hershey were popular with many groups. During the postwar years the rose display reached its height with 42,000 rose bushes of 1,200 varieties.

Panel Disussion Group of Rose Experts at Conard-Pyle Company's Star Rose Gardens, September 10, 1949. Harry Erdman's reputation as a rose expert continued to grow along with that of the Rose Garden (Erdman, designer and superintendent of the Hershey Rose Garden, is 2nd from the left.)

Envelope with National Rose Show Postmark, 1952. The 15th anniversary of the Rose Garden was celebrated in Hershey with a national rose show sponsored by the Penn-Jersey District of the American Rose Society. More than 6,000 visitors came on the first day alone to see over 2,000 entries from the United States, Cuba and Canada—and, of course, to visit the Hershey Rose Garden.

Rose Queen Crowning Ceremony, June 1953. To help celebrate the 50th anniversary of the town in 1953, a statewide contest for a Rose Queen was held. The contest climaxed in Hershey with the crowning of the queen and several days of associated festivities. The man in the picture is Pennsylvania Governor John Fine.

John Mezaros, Gardens Director (on right), with Henry Hohman, of Kingsville Nursery, 1971. Mezaros was in charge of the garden from 1957-1975. During his tenure he added many new plant collections. The largest of these was a donation of hundreds of rare and unusual trees and shrubs from Henry Hohman, an internationally known plant propagator from Maryland.

Reflecting Pond with Swans and Roses, 1960's. Throughout most of the 1950's and 1960's swans were kept on the reflecting pond. Even though the birds are long gone, it is still referred to as "Swan Lake" by local citizens.

Leone Gerberich Pruning Climbing Rose, ca. 1990's. Gerberich was hired in 1953 and remained with the garden for over 40 years. During that time he became head of maintenance and an award-winning rosarian. His work with the roses was an important factor in the first-class reputation of the Rose Garden over the years.

GUIDED TOUR HERSHEY ROSE GARDENS & ARBORETUM

Hershey, Pennsylvania 17033

Weeping Beech Being Unloaded, 1967. Because of the on-going addition of interesting trees to the garden, its name was changed to Hershey Rose Gardens and Arboretum in 1965.

Tulip Time, 1950's. Each spring when 30,000 tulips bloomed, employees in Dutch costume walked among the flower beds to be available for photographs and to raise funds for the garden by taking bulb orders from visitors.

Easter Sunrise Service, 1973. Local churches took turns presenting the service, with music provided by a brass ensemble of local high school students. These services became a tradition in postwar years and beyond. The memory of attending them is still cherished by many Hershey residents.

FOUR

Survival and Progress in Difficult Times: 1970 – 1989

Many attempts were made to move the Hershey Rose Garden towards financial independence during the 1970's and 1980's. An admission fee was instituted in 1973. In order to increase visitation, significant horticultural improvements were added and visitor amenities were increased. The greatest of these changes was the creation, in 1979, of six attractive theme gardens on the grounds to complement the rose area. At the same time a new name, Hershey Gardens, was adopted to emphasize these multiple attractions.

In the 1980's a variety of interpretive and cultural programming was initiated, along with a renewed emphasis on restoring high standards of horticultural excellence. But by 1987, its 50th anniversary year, it was clear that no amount of effort and creativity was going to enable the garden to generate enough revenue to cover its expenses—it's a rare public garden that can. There was even serious consideration of closing it down altogether.

However, in 1989 a solution was found. Responsibility for the garden was transferred from the for-profit Hershey Entertainment and Resorts Company to a small foundation created by Milton Hershey to support educational and cultural institutions in the community. The M.S. Hershey Foundation was able to provide capital for much needed modernization of the garden's infrastructure as well as to assure enough yearly operating funds for survival.

Colonial Garden, May 1984. This was one of the theme gardens that was created on Rose Garden property as a means of attracting larger numbers of visitors.

Hershey Rose Gardens and Arboretum Entry Sign, First Year of Admission Fee, 1973. Many Hershey residents found the fee—plus the fence that was put up around the property—hard to accept. They had always thought of the garden as a special gift to them from Milton Hershey.

Bill Bowman, Director, 1975-1984. Bowman added the theme gardens in 1979. These not only provided a more varied visitor experience but also consolidated some of the plant collections.

Design for New Hershey Gardens Logo, 1979. With the addition of the themed areas, roses were no longer the main focal point of the garden. To reflect the change in emphasis, the name was changed to Hershey Gardens and a logo with a stylized tulip was adopted.

Rock Garden Construction, 1979. HERCO, Inc., which had responsibility for the garden at the time, invested heavily in the construction of the theme gardens as well as in the marketing necessary to bring them to the attention of the public.

Theme Garden Locations, 1979. After two years of planning, construction and planting, the theme gardens were completed in June 1979. At first, these beautiful attractions caused an increase in visitation. However, times were changing. Attendance dropped steadily during the 1980's, compounding the garden's financial difficulties.

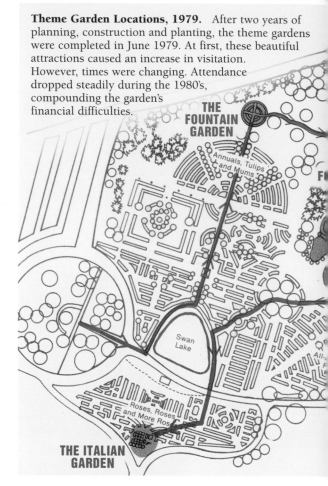

Tiny Tim Concert in Hershey Gardens, May 1982. The tulip display proved to be the perfect place for Tiny Tim, popular TV entertainer, to perform his famous rendition of "Tiptoe Through the Tulips."

Mark Gruin with Gardens' 50th Birthday Cake, 1987. Originally hired in 1983 to start cultural and educational programming, Gruin became director in 1985. Besides public programming, he instituted involvement of community volunteers and the development of a membership base—all new directions for the gardens.

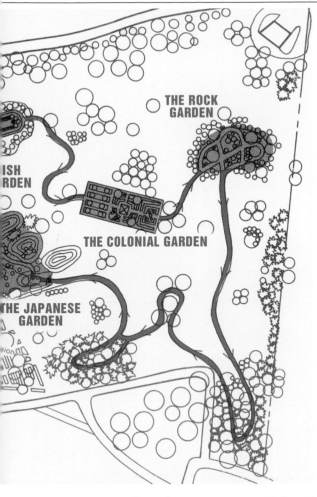

Jazz Concert in the Oak Grove, 1980's. The jazz series and other cultural programming started in this era provided a whole new way for people to enjoy the gardens. Programming was not cost effective and could not be continued due to the garden's limited operating budget, but it was popular with the public.

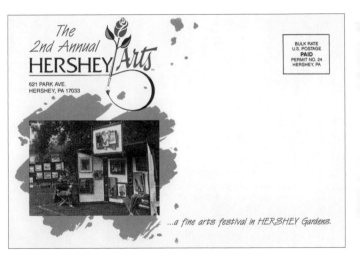

Hershey Arts Festival Brochure, 1987. A juried show that included both art and entertainment, "HersheyArts" was held at the gardens annually from 1986 to 1989.

Hershey Gardens at 50 still had a fine reputation in the horticultural world.

Tulips in Hershey Gardens, 1987. Each spring the gardens had a dazzling display of 30,000 to 40,000 blooming tulips.

Hershey Gardens Roses, 1987. An article in the 1989 *American Rose Annual* stated, "Hershey Gardens has established an international reputation in the botanical world. Its seasonal plantings and themed gardens beckon enthusiasts of all interests. For the rosarian, Hershey Gardens should be an obligatory pilgrimage site."

FIVE

Revitalization: 1990 – 2005

The most recent history of the Hershey Gardens has been one of renewal and new directions. With its survival assured by the M.S. Hershey Foundation, the gardens was ready to be moved beyond a maintenance mode. Because funding was limited, however, it was not an easy task to figure out how, and the Foundation turned to the community for assistance. A volunteer advisory board of local citizens committed to the welfare of the gardens was formed.

The activities of this board proved to be central to the revitalization that began in the 1990's. The board spearheaded innovative projects which, in turn, attracted other volunteers who were eager to help. Since that time, volunteer assistance with many functions from long-range planning and fundraising to gardening has become integral to the operation of the gardens. With the help of board planning it also became possible to take the necessary step of building a creative and professional staff. These factors, added to the solid basis of Foundation support, have resulted in many improvements including restoration of a large part of the original rose garden, development of two major new attractions—the Butterfly House and the Children's Garden—plus re-introduction of educational programming and public events. With increased audience appeal, visitation has grown dramatically and more funding sources have become available. The late 20th and early 21st Centuries have proven to be a productive and exciting time for Hershey Gardens.

Entrance to Butterfly House and Children's Garden, August 2005. These two new attractions, plus many other improvements, have helped to bring increasing numbers of visitors.

Greeting Attendees at the First Gardenfest, Sept. 22, 1996.
David L. Parke, Jr., Gardens Executive Director from 1990–2004 (seen here on the left), encouraged a group of interested community members to form a gardens advisory board in 1995. Their first venture was a day-long Gardenfest sponsored jointly with the Hershey-Derry Township Historical Society and the Hershey Horticulture Society. This free event, with family activities and many booths representing non-profit community organizations, has become an annual affair.

Restored Rose Garden, 1997. The 60th anniversary of the Hershey Rose Garden was celebrated with renovations of the original structures and new plantings, including the addition of 2,000 rose bushes to help restore the rose area to its original design. The Conard-Pyle Company, who had supplied many of the roses in the fall of 1936, donated 1,345 of the new bushes planted during the restoration. Volunteers were instrumental in the development and completion of this project.

Barbara Whitcraft, Director of Horticulture, 2005. Since joining the Gardens staff in 1996, Whitcraft has brought renewed vitality to the landscaping in all areas of the Gardens.

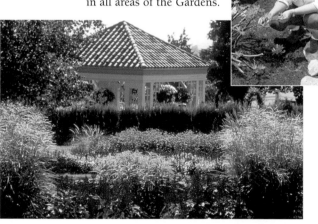

"Cool Color" Annuals, 1998. One of Whitcraft's specialties is the brilliant display of mixed annuals which take the place of the tulips in late spring and brighten the gardens over the long summer season.

New Rock Garden Path, 1998. Pathways to make exploring the gardens easier for all visitors, including the disabled, were added in the late 1990's.

Volunteers Planting Tulip Bulbs, Oct. 1999. Since the mid-1990's volunteers have helped staff gardeners to get planting done in a timely manner and to keep plants looking neat and trim throughout the growing season.

Butterfly House, Exterior, 2000. A brainchild of the gardens advisory board, the Butterfly House was one of ten such attractions in the nation when it opened in 1998.

Butterfly House, Interior, 1999. The arches that support the mesh screen of the butterfly house were originally part of a greenhouse that was built for Milton Hershey in 1930.

Education Building, 2003. For the first time in its history, the gardens now has both indoor space and sheltered outdoor space for classes and meetings, thanks to the Education Building constructed in conjunction with the Children's Garden.

Children's Garden Ribbon Cutting, Spring 2003. Advisory board and staff worked closely for two years to create the Children's Garden. The $1.5 million project was primarily funded by local and regional individuals and businesses.

Deer's-eye View of Tulip Beds, 2005. In the 1990's deer caused large-scale destruction of the tulip beds in spite of multiple efforts to keep them away. For several years no tulips at all were planted. Then, in 1997, the problem was solved by the erection of the fence that surrounds 13 acres of the main garden area.

Bill Bowman Garden, Fall 2005. This statue is the focal point of a memorial garden built in the main display area with funds donated by Bowman's friends and family. Former director Bowman, acting as a volunteer board member, played a key role in the revitalization of the gardens from 1995 to the time of his death in 2004.

Tai Chi Class, 2005. Hershey Gardens provides a serene setting for Tai Chi, Yoga and other fitness classes. The number and variety of classes offered to adults and children have grown steadily in the 2000's.

Hershey Rose Garden and Hotel Hershey, Hershey, Pa.

1938

2005

SIX

The Constant Garden

Many aspects of the entrance, rose and seasonal gardens that delighted visitors in the late 1930's and early 1940's may be seen in the garden today. Formal beds separated by lawn pathways are still used to display thousands of roses, tulips and annuals. Panoramic views towards the chocolate factory and town to the south and Hotel Hershey to the north continue to be part of the charm of the garden's location. The pond remains in its original size and shape, encircled with red roses as it has been since the garden opened. Structures such as the tile-roofed gazebo, large trellis bench and small, pillared sales building look the same now as when they were first built. Even some of the statues and garden ornaments that were installed in the earliest years can be found in their initial locations.

There have, of course, been some changes in these features over the years. Today the view towards town includes new buildings, amusement park rides and an enlarged chocolate factory. The hotel is now almost hidden by trees that have grown to maturity. The number of formal beds has periodically waxed and waned. Varieties and cultivars of tulips, annuals and roses have been replaced with new, improved ones as they came on the market and earlier types became unavailable. The gazebo and trellis bench have been covered to greater and lesser degrees with climbers.

The overall look and feel of these features, however, have remained remarkably constant. Thus, they provide today's visitors with a direct connection to Hershey Gardens past.

Hershey Rose Garden and Hotel Hershey, Hershey, Pa.

1951

Views Towards Hotel Hershey from Hershey Gardens, Then and Now. A time traveler who had visited the Rose Garden in earlier years would have no difficulty in recognizing this view today.

Originally known as the pergola, and now as the gazebo, this structure was designed to be a shady place for visitors to relax and admire the view over the rose beds and pond. Although the nomenclature has changed, this little building has not. Still located on its rose-covered hill, it continues to provide a welcome place for visitors to rest and enjoy the scenery. With the passing of time it has become a Hershey Gardens landmark.

Gazebo Under Construction, 1936 – 1937

Gazebo, 2005

ca. 1960

"The Boy with the Leaking Boot."
Purchased in 1913, this fountain enlivened the first Hershey Park swimming pool and later one of the Hershey Zoo buildings before being stored under the Park dance hall. In the late 1930's Milton Hershey requested that it be placed in the Rose Garden. It was then refurbished and set up by the pond where it has remained for many years with a few brief periods elsewhere in the gardens.

A replica of the original fountain may be seen today in its initial gardens location. The original was restored in 1997, but remained too fragile to go back outside and was placed in the Hershey Museum.

2005

"Rebecca at the Well," 2005.
This statue was originally purchased for the High Point Mansion grounds in 1913. Located at first in front of the mansion, it later graced a small island in a pond on the property. When the pond became neglected after Catherine Hershey's death, the statue broke at the base and fell into the water. It was rescued and eventually brought to its present location in the garden in 1938. Ever since that time Rebecca has been in the same place, encircled by roses.

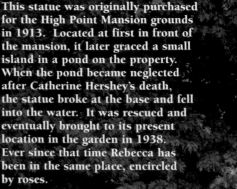

1937   **Rose Garden Beds**   2005

Formal beds surrounded by lawn have been the key design element of the rose and seasonal gardens since the early years of the garden. Today, many of the beds are in their original locations.

Through the Arch of Roses is seen the
Biblical Bronze Statue of Rebecca with Water Jar
On her way to the Reflecting Pool

1951

Northeast View of Rebecca Statue, 1951 and 2005.
From this vantage point Rebecca seems poised to make
her way down the hill to get water from the garden
pond. This view of the statue has been popular with
photographers for many years.

2005

Built in the grove of trees
overlooking the rose beds in
1938, the year after the garden
opened, this structure has been
used continuously as a shop for
garden visitors. It became an
admissions building as well after
fees were instituted in 1973 and
at times has even provided staff
office space. Its Doric columns,
pleasing proportions and
lofty location have made it
a harmonious part of
the landscape since it
was constructed.

Sales Building, ca. 1948

Sales/Admissions Building, 2005

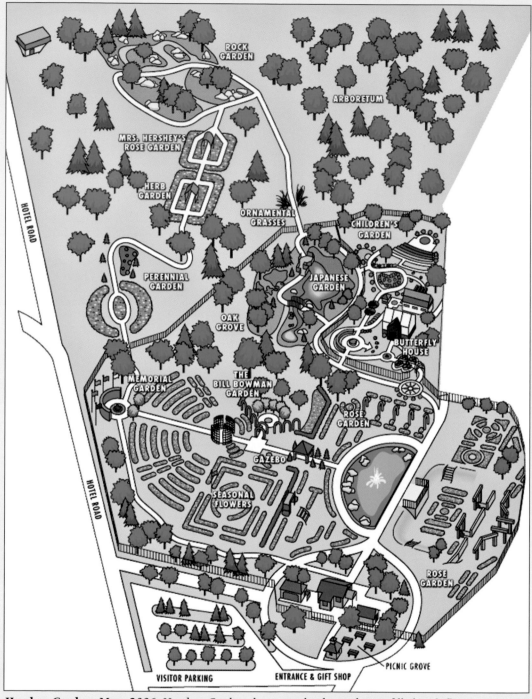

Hershey Gardens Map, 2006. Hershey Gardens has many landscaped areas filled with flowers, trees and shrubs plus a Butterfly House and Children's Garden. The Gardens Today section of this book takes the reader on a tour that emphasizes both the aesthetic and the practical aspects of gardening to be found there.

THE GARDENS TODAY

"Certainly, the Garden is a living, growing, magnificent tribute to the founder, M. S. Hershey, and a blessing of beauty to the people he loved."

– John Mezaros, Director, Hershey Rose Garden, 1957-1975.

SEVEN

Entrance Garden

The entrance to Hershey Gardens is set on a knoll in a stand dominated by native trees that were already mature when the Rose Garden opened in 1937. Four kinds of oak—chestnut, saw-tooth, scarlet and white, plus white ash and tulip poplar—still remain here in what had once been a farm wood-lot. Their trunks now soar up forty feet or more, branching out into an overarching canopy. In the summer this stand is thick with leaves that sift the sunlight into dappled patches on the smaller trees, shrubs and herbaceous plants that cluster around the entrance buildings and spill down the side of the hill.

As visitors leave the entrance buildings and walk towards the main display areas, the trunks and branches of the woody vegetation frame successive views of the gardens—the lake surrounded by roses with the colorful Children's Garden gate and the white glow of the Butterfly House in the distance; the fountain sending cascades of sparkling drops into the water below; the blaze of thousands of tulips in the spring and the blues, pinks and purples of the "cool-colored" annual beds later in the season; the shady, tile-roofed gazebo set in the midst of brilliant flowers; a row of brightly colored hanging baskets along the side of a roadway and paths leading past groupings of specimen trees. All of these entice visitors to make their way out of the entrance area to experience the joys of exploring Hershey Gardens.

View Towards Tulip Beds from the Entrance Garden, Mid-Spring. New tree leaves cast delicate shadows on entrance garden shrubbery, making a pleasant contrast with the sun-lit tulip beds in the distance.

Introductory Views of the Main Gardens

A path from the main entrance building runs along the side of the hill towards the display areas. It provides glimpses through the trees of what the visitor will soon be seeing close up.

Lake Fountain, Mid-Spring.
The play of the water in the fountain adds ever-changing patterns to the view.

Gardens Pond, Late Spring.
'Red Fountain' large-flowering climber roses cover the fence that encircles the pond. Beyond it are the Children's Garden gate and the Butterfly House.

Pedestrian Roadway, Late Summer. Another path goes straight down the hill and joins a roadway that bisects the rose gardens. It ends at the Children's Garden gate. Visitors are free to leave paths at any time to walk on the lawns surrounding the flower beds.

Woodland Trail, Early Summer. A short, grassy trail meanders through the trees between the two pathways. Where it joins the hillside path there is a view of bright flowers bordered and backed by groupings of trees.

Upper Rose Garden, Early Summer.
The green-roofed gazebo is the focal point in this garden.

Entrance Garden Hillside, Mid-Spring. After entering the gardens, a look back up the hill provides the best view of the massed plantings of azaleas and rhododendrons there.

EIGHT

Tulips and Other Spring Bulbs

The first big floral display each year starts in late April when the tulips begin to bloom, and by early May the tulip beds are ablaze with color. Single and double, with petals pointed, rounded, striped, or fringed—30,000 tulips of more than 100 different varieties fill the formal beds on the north side of the gardens.

All Hershey Gardens tulips are grown from premium bulbs imported from Holland. They are planted unusually close together, which intensifies the colors. Planting is done at the end of October in beds with leaf mulch tilled into them. After having been planted with tulips for three years in a row, each bed is given a rest in order to help prevent soil-borne diseases. Weeding and removal of dead flowers keep the beds looking their best. When the bloom is over, the bulbs are removed and annuals are planted in their place. New tulip bulbs are used each year.

In contrast to the formality of the tulip beds, other spring bulbs including winter aconites, blue scillas, assorted narcissus, hyacinths, wood hyacinths and alliums are set, along with perennials and shrubs, in smaller areas scattered throughout the gardens. These plantings are designed to show amateur gardeners the kinds of effects that can be obtained with spring bulbs in the more informal settings of home gardens.

Tulip Display, Mid-Spring. Thousands of tulips light up the seasonal beds with shades of purple, red, yellow, orange and pink. Darwin hybrid and lily-flowered varieties are in the foreground. The yellow and red flowers seen in the middle beds are bouquet tulips, with single stalks bearing multiple blooms.

Single Late and Darwin Tulips at Sunset, Mid-Spring. The long rays of the sun give the flowers a luminous quality as though there were a sunset glowing in the tulip beds.

First Bulbs of the Season to Bloom, Early Spring. On a dull March day, bright yellow winter aconites, *Eranthis hyemalis*, look like concentrated patches of sunshine under the trees of the Entrance Garden. The Lenten rose, *Helleborus orientalis*, at the bottom left, is an early bloomer that grows from rootstocks, not bulbs. It also helps to herald the coming of spring at Hershey Gardens.

East End of the Gardens, Mid-Spring. The color of hyacinth 'Splendid Cornelia' seems to be repeated by clouds of flowering plum and magnolia blossoms in the late afternoon sunlight.

Perennial Garden, Mid-Spring. Shiny-leaved 'P.J.M.' rhododendrons with their profusion of lavender flowers provide a back-drop for slender-stalked daffodils.

Late Spring Ground Cover. Wood hyacinths, *Scilla campanulata*, have been planted under trees near the entrance to the Japanese Garden. Their stalks of soft, nodding pastel blossoms provide an interesting contrast to the bright, stiff azaleas in the background.

Tulips in Full Bloom, Mid-Spring. Large blocks of color in a concentric pattern give the effect of a magnificent, brilliantly patterned carpet.

On a Perfect Day, Mid-Spring. New leaves, flowering trees and green lawns surround the tulip beds with their brightly colored, silky flowers.

NINE

Rose Gardens

Seven thousand rose bushes blooming simultaneously and in profusion surround visitors to the Hershey Gardens with color and scent in late May and early June.

Dramatic masses of color are created by assigning one variety to each of the shorter beds and only two or three varieties to each of the longer ones. The beds are laid out in a formal design that is punctuated with arches and pillars covered with blossoms. Continuous, although less heavy, bloom brightens the rose beds during the rest of the summer, with one last, heavier burst of color that dwindles slowly as cold weather approaches.

Ever since the Hershey Rose Garden first opened in 1937 it has featured many types of roses at the same time. This practice provides diversity of form and height which adds to the beauty of the display. It also serves to introduce visitors to the kinds of roses that are available and should perform well in their own gardens.

Most of the roses grown in the Hershey Gardens are All America Rose Selection (AARS) winners. This means that before a species is planted it has won a top rating during a rigorous two-year testing process that most of the new species entered by breeders must undergo. Only one to four roses a year are awarded this honor. Hershey Gardens, an accredited AARS display garden, grows recent winners as well as those from past years.

Lower Rose Garden, Mid-Spring. 'New Dawn' climbers, just coming into bloom on garden trellises, create a luxuriant frame for beds of roses in the distance and a rich background for the mass of pink 'Carefree Beauty' floribunda blossoms which surround the birdbath.

**'Parade'
Climber and
View, Late
Spring.**
The 'Parade'
large-flowered
climbers on
either side of
this arch were
planted in
1953, and still
bloom profusely
each spring.

Miniature Roses in the Late Summer Garden. Beds of miniature roses
make cheerful ribbons of color in front of trellises covered with the
small white flowers of Sweet Autumn Clematis, *Clematis paniculata*,
vines. Hershey Gardens has been one of the American Rose Society's
test gardens for miniature roses since the 1980's.

**View from the
Upper Rose
Garden, Early
Summer.**
Slanting rays
of early morn-
ing sun high-
light the
clusters of
fiery, orange-
red 'Impatient'
floribunda
blooms in
a bed overlook-
ing the lower
rose garden.

On a Mid-Spring Afternoon. The garden provides a serene setting for a leisurely walk among the roses. The rose bed in the front of the picture is planted with 'Friendship', a hybrid tea that was an All American Rose winner in 1979.

View to the Southeast, Mid-Spring. The gazebo, with 'Eden' large-flowered climbers at its corners, is located half-way up the hill in the center of the upper gardens. Views from all sides of it offer a panorama of the surrounding rose-filled acreage.

Upper Rose Garden, Late Spring. When the rose bloom is at its height, the garden is radiant with the opulent colors and sheer abundance of velvet-textured blossoms.

TEN

Annuals

As full summer approaches, rose bloom is less heavy in the gardens and the major display of color shifts to the annual beds. Located on the one-acre slope above the rose gardens, where the tulips are to be seen in the spring, the rectangular and curved beds make bold geometric patterns against the green of the lawn. Soft and cool colors—blues, lavenders and pinks—predominate in the section closest to the entrance garden. The beds here form concentric squares around a central ring. An adjoining area of equal size to the northeast has beds radiating in a fan shape which blaze with hot colors—reds, oranges and yellows.

The overall artistic effect of the beds is achieved by careful use of contrasts. Plant size and shape, plus textures, shapes, colors and sizes of flowers and leaves are all taken into consideration. Of equal importance are the horticultural properties of the plant materials. Growth patterns, time and length of bloom, hardiness and resistance to disease are factored into the choice of genus, species and cultivar.

Planting is done in mid-May after thorough soil preparation. Leaf compost is tilled into the soil before planting and is also used for mulch. Fertilizer is used at planting time, and a foliar feed of liquid fertilizer is applied after a few weeks. During the remainder of the summer, each species of plant is fed according to its individual needs. Consistent watering and weeding keep the beds in top condition well into October.

Cool and Hot Color Annual Beds, Late Summer.
A rich tapestry of colors is provided all summer long in the seasonal section of the gardens by 12,650 annual plants representing 125 cultivars.

The Gardens Today

Mid-Summer Morning. Early morning light intensifies the shapes and colors in the beds.

Harmonious Mixture, Mid-Summer. The pointed grey-green leaves of *Celosia spicata* 'Flamingo Purple' seen here at the right provide an interesting contrast with the surrounding leaves and flowers.

Late Summer Morning. Spikes covered with miniature flowers make airy clouds of blue, pink, purple and white. These mingle with patches of deeper shades of the same colors made by larger blossoms.

Late Summer Afternoon. Lofty orange 'Wyoming' and reddish 'Black Knight' cannas and tall purple fountain grass, *Pennisetum setaceum* 'Rubrum,' preside over flame-colored flowers of lower-growing annuals.

Evening Light, Late Summer. *Celosia cristata* 'Castle Orange,' *Solenostenum scutellarioides* 'Wizard Autumn' coleus and *Tagetes patula* 'Aurora Orange' marigold appear to glow with their own internal light as the sun's rays lengthen.

Yellow and White Combinations, Early Summer. Visitors enjoy strolling on the lawn pathways between the beds where shades of yellow, cream and white swirl together.

Perennial Garden

Herb Garden

Mrs. Hershey's Rose Garden

Rock Garden

ELEVEN

Along the Garden Path

A path north of the big display gardens guides visitors eastward through four smaller, more intimate gardens and a larger rock garden, all surrounded with lawns and shaded by a variety of specimen trees and shrubs.

The Perennial Garden comes first. Here, an oval brick walk is bordered by deep beds backed with shrubs and filled with native and exotic species. The sequence of color starts with rhododendrons and daffodils in the spring and lasts well into the fall.

The path then winds through a woody area to the Herb Garden. Its small gazebo, which has been in the Gardens almost from the beginning, is surrounded by a colorful and aromatic rectangle of old-fashioned plants once grown by Native Americans and early Pennsylvanians for such purposes as cooking, medicines and dye-making.

Mrs. Hershey's Rose Garden, with highly fragrant, old-fashioned varieties, is only a few feet down the path. This garden was moved here from the Hershey Mansion in 1942.

The Rock Garden follows, with the path making a loop through needle-leaved evergreens, hollies, boxwoods and dogwoods, some of them quite rare. Small areas of spring bulbs, perennials and flowering shrubs add color to this setting of rocks and greenery.

Before the path meets the gate at the Japanese Garden, it passes through an area with large clumps of ornamental grasses, many of which reach eight to ten feet.

View from the Perennial Garden Path, Late Spring.
A look back towards the main display area and entrance garden reveals a scene that captures the vigor and freshness of the season. Trees with bright spring foliage surround the Perennial Garden which is just starting to burst into bloom.

Weeping Beech Gateway to the Path, Early Summer.
The path leading out of the main display area goes through a tunnel under a large weeping beech, *Fagus sylvaticus* 'pendula'. The open gate at the tunnel's end invites the visitor to explore what lies beyond.

Perennial Garden, Early Summer.
Shasta daisy, *Chrysanthemum x superbum*; whorled tickseed, *Coreopsis verticillata* 'zagreb;' sages, *Salvia x superba* 'May night' and *Salvia verticillata* 'purple rain,' plus red-hot poker, *Kniphofia uvaria*, are early favorites in this garden.

Ornamental Grasses, Late Fall.
An attraction for both the eyes and the ears, these grasses shimmer as they catch the light, and rustle and whisper in even the lightest of breezes.

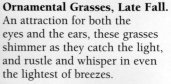

Herb Garden, Late Fall. Marigolds, *Tagetes tenuifolia* 'Golden Gem' and 'Lemon Gem,' whose petals can be used for dying fabric, brighten up this late fall scene.

Mrs. Hershey's Rose Garden, Late Spring. The pink 'American Beauty' climber on the right of the trellis is one of two remaining plants from the 1942 Hershey Mansion rose garden. The other roses in this garden are newer plants of the same old rose varieties that had been in the original garden. These were installed when the garden was restored in the late 1960's.

Path to Herb Garden, Late Spring. The visitor may wander on the lawn between the trees, rest on one of the benches or continue on the path towards the Herb Garden.

Rock Garden, Early Fall. Multiple textures, shapes and colors of trees and shrubs make dramatic contrasts in this wooded area.

TWELVE

Japanese Garden

Elements of Japanese style have been used in this garden to provide a cool and peaceful retreat with an Asian feeling. Stones and water are as important as the vegetation here. All three are carefully situated to give the visitor a heightened awareness of different aspects of nature. Permanence is represented by the stones that edge the central pond and help to define its banks. The motion of the water in the stream that feeds the pond is a reminder of the passage of time. Evergreens, which make up the majority of the trees, provide a living framework for the water. They also make a stable background for the deciduous trees, shrubs and herbaceous plants whose aspect varies throughout the year. These are used sparingly in order to draw attention to their individual characteristics as they highlight the changing of the seasons. Reflections of sky, stones and plants in the pond heighten the effect of this harmonious landscape.

The bridge that crosses the pond and the narrow pathways that wind through the plantings provide views over the water and are an invitation for visitors to take their time to enjoy the beauty and tranquility of this garden.

Japanese Garden Pond, Mid-Spring. Reflections in the pond double the effect of the landscaping around it—the large, arching, flower-laden Beautybush, *Kolkwitzia amabilis*, isolated patches of deep-blue Siberian iris, *Iris Siberica*, irregular grey stones and many unusual trees and shrubs.

The Gardens Today

Winter. Snow highlights the straight lines of the bridge and softens the outlines of the branches with "snow blossoms," or "sekku," the Japanese name for the snow that settles on trees.

Summer. The Japanese Garden provides a cool and serene oasis that offsets the intensity of light and color elsewhere in the gardens. An interesting Hershey note is that the granite paving stones seen here were originally used as liners in the bottom of mixing machines in the early chocolate factory.

Spring.
Bright blooming azaleas are used here, as they often are in more traditional Japanese gardens, to provide a vivid contrast to the background of multiple shades and textures of green and brown.

Fall.
Deciduous trees are used sparingly in this garden in order to emphasize the brilliance of each one's autumn foliage.

THIRTEEN

Trees and Shrubs

The tall trees in the grove that surrounds the entrance of the Hershey Gardens are well over 100 years old. These were the only trees of any consequence on either of the original two parcels of land that form the present-day gardens. Since then, more than 400 trees and shrubs representing several hundred species have been added, singly and in groups, throughout the property.

From the towering stand of blue atlas cedars, *Cedrus atlantica* 'Glauca,' which can be seen from almost anywhere in the gardens, to the low-growing sweetbox, *Sarcococca hookeriana*, shrubs that act as ground cover in a corner of the Japanese Garden, the multiple sizes, shapes, textures and colors of woody plants add interest, structure and diversity to the landscape. They frame many views, help to demarcate areas and provide background contrast for the herbaceous plants and lawns. Visitors find welcome shade under the trees on hot summer days.

Collections of weeping trees, hollies and Japanese maples, plus a variety of unusual woody species and cultivars, provide horticultural interest as well as beauty. Native trees and shrubs are mingled with those that have origins in distant parts of the world. Spring, when scores of them are covered with bright blossoms, and autumn, when many display brilliantly colored leaves, are the showiest times for trees and shrubs in the gardens, but they are a vital part of the landscape throughout the year.

Early Morning, Mid-Summer. Sunlight filters through the branches of trees in the arboretum section of the gardens where many large and unusual specimens are to be found.

The Gardens Today

Blue Atlas Cedars, *Cedrus atlantica* 'Glauca,' **Early Summer.**
The soft, blue-grey tones of the centrally located stand of lofty blue atlas cedars make a complementary background for views of bright flowers.

Japanese Snowbell,
Styrax japonicus '**Pink Chimes,**' **Late Spring.**
The drooping, bell-like flowers that crowd the branches of this unusual species, perfume the surrounding air with a delicate fragrance.

Magnolia Grove, Early Spring. Magnolia blossoms of light and dark pink, white and even one unusual yellow variety are among the first flowers to appear.

Weeping Blue Atlas Cedar, *Cedrus atlantica* 'Glauca Pendula,' **Mid-Fall.** Hershey Gardens has a fine collection of weeping trees. This specimen is so large that its branches must be held off the ground with wooden props.

Oak-Leaved Hydrangeas, *Hydrangea quercifolia,* **and Annuals in the Entrance Garden, Early Summer.** Shrubs are used in many parts of the gardens to add an interesting and colorful backdrop in beds and groupings of plants.

Arboretum View, Mid-Fall. The large willow oak, *Quercus phellos,* to the right is just one of the many arboretum trees which were planted in the early 1940's and have now reached their full height.

Ginkgo Trees, *Ginkgo biloba,* **Late Fall.** The bright yellow leaves of these trees drop almost simultaneously, making a golden carpet on the ground.

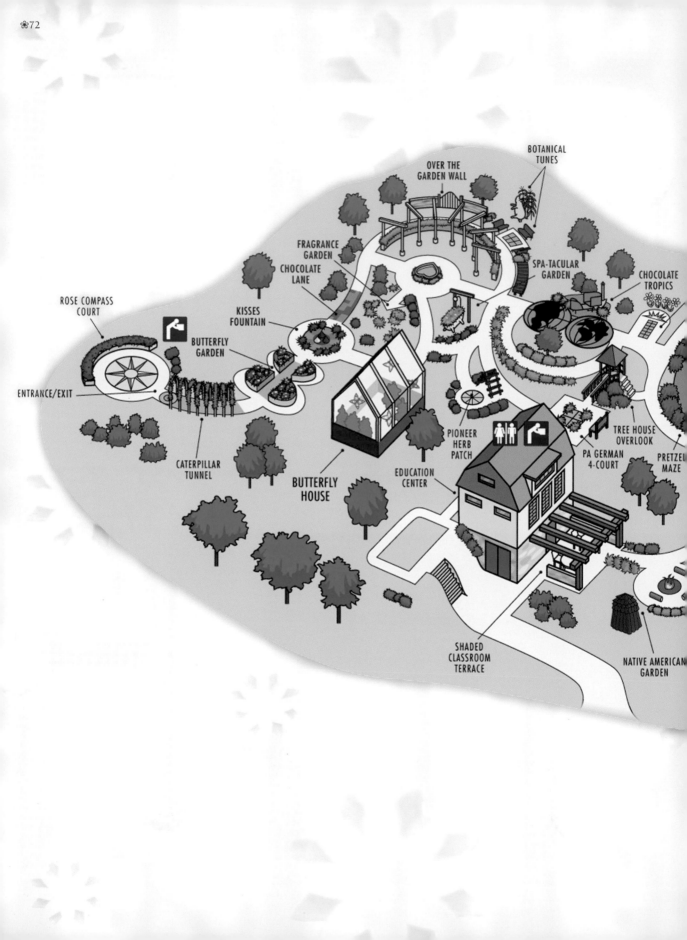

FOURTEEN

Children's Garden

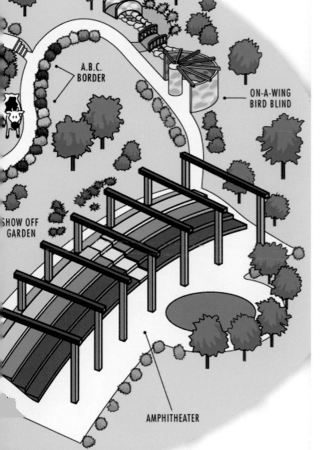

The Children's Garden is a space unlike any other in Hershey Gardens. It was designed to appeal to the young and the young at heart, and is an environment that encourages the exuberance, sense of wonder and vivid imagination of its smallest visitors. Opportunities for them to interact with their accompanying grownups are plentiful.

Bright colors abound, and this one-and-a-half acre garden is filled to overflowing. There are fountains, statuary that can be climbed on, a butterfly house, interactive exhibits and an amphitheater, as well as indoor and outdoor classrooms. One of the major purposes of the garden is to introduce children to the fascination and beauty of the horticultural world. Five-hundred species of plants, including 40 kinds of trees and shrubs, are an integral part of the design.

The garden is organized into themed areas that reflect young children's tastes, interests and attention spans. These areas can be entered from the path that winds its way down a gentle slope. Some of the themes are universal. Among these are the botanical tunes area, the tree house, and the river banker's picnic area. Some, such as the Native American and Pennsylvania German gardens and the chocolate-oriented areas, are tied more directly to central Pennsylvania and Hershey. Other areas such as the A.B.C. border, the human sundial and the compass court offer more specific learning experiences. All of the areas, however, provide visitors of all ages the chance to enjoy themselves in a relaxed and welcoming atmosphere.

Children's Garden Map. The different areas within the Children's Garden offer many opportunities for active play and learning.

Say hello to a friendly bee.

Make up stories.

Admire the flowers.

Here are some of the things you can do in the Children's Garden

Have a tea party.

Grind corn the old-fashioned way.

Play the xylophone.

Watch the birds.

Listen to a story in the tree house.

Ride a pig…

…and give him a hug.

Put on a show for your family.

Enjoy the misty spray from the kiss fountains.

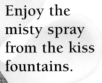

Pretend to cook a meal outdoors

Sail a boat in the chocolate tropics.

Play the alligator drum.

Hide under a weeping beech tree.

Smell the mint...

...and let Maizie the cow smell it too.

Dance on the dance chimes.

Play hide and seek in the pretzel maze.

See how long the ball will stay up.

Check out the alphabet garden.

Dream on the river bank bridge.

FIFTEEN

Butterfly House

From late May through late September, the 30 by 50 foot mesh-covered Butterfly House is open to the public. By mid-summer as many as 400 butterflies, representing more than 25 North American species, may be seen there. The house is designed to provide the best possible environment for the butterflies as well as a pleasant and interesting experience for their visitors. It is located in the Children's Garden in a sunny spot where the butterflies can be the most active and comfortable. Inside the house, plants with brightly colored, nectar-producing flowers grow on either side of a brick pathway that curves around a small pond.

Visitors can watch up close as butterflies sip nectar, feed on over-ripe fruit, bask in the sun, hover and fly silently by on their brilliantly patterned, velvety wings.

The whole life cycle of butterflies may be seen in the house. Some lay eggs on special plants provided for them. The caterpillars that hatch feed on the leaves and then turn into chrysalids (where they transform into butterflies). However, the majority of the house butterflies emerge from the 100 or more chrysalids that are purchased each week from butterfly farms. These chrysalids can be observed in a glass-fronted case as they mature and the butterflies emerge. Volunteer "flight attendants" and staff are stationed at the case and at other locations in the house to discuss the butterflies and answer visitors' questions.

Entry Garden to the Butterfly House. Visitors reach the house (seen here at the right) by walking through a caterpillar-like, vine-covered tunnel onto a pathway decorated as a butterfly body complete with eyes and antennae. The raised, wing-shaped flower beds on either side are crowded with brightly colored flowers filled with nectar that is irresistible to butterflies.

Butterfly House Walkway. Only plants known to be especially attractive to butterflies are grown in the house. All are suitable for growing in home gardens.

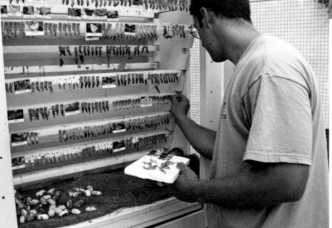

Replenishing the Chrysalis Case. An intern pins a shipment of chrysalids into neat rows. Moth cocoons are lying on the shelf at the lower left.

Chrysalids and Newly Emerged Butterflies. When a butterfly emerges it pumps fluid into the veins in its crumpled wings. After an hour or more the wings become strong enough for flight and the new butterfly is ready to be released into the house.

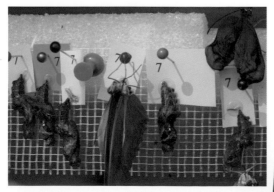

Butterflies Visiting Visitors. Occasionally a butterfly will land on a lucky visitor.

Butterfly House Pond. The first thing that visitors see when they enter the house is this pond surrounded by lush vegetation and multi-colored flowers. Butterflies hover over the flowers and sip nectar from them.

Caterpillars Explained. A volunteer "flight attendant" helps visitors to understand caterpillar behavior and the butterfly life cycle.

A Food for Every Taste. Those species that prefer to feed on rotting fruit have their own place to feast. The handsome pedestal for the feeder dish is a granite roller from a mixing machine used in the early days of the Hershey chocolate factory.

Caterpillar Boxes.
A continuous supply of fresh leaves is provided for the hungry inhabitants of these "munch boxes."

SIXTEEN

Winter in the Gardens

Winter is a quiet time in the gardens. The bustle of summer visitors is over and the gardeners are mainly indoors. For the plants it is a resting period when growth nearly comes to a standstill. A multitude of adaptations helps them to survive the rigors of the season. But for many species the cold is not just a test of endurance. They must have the months of chill in order to develop properly when the weather starts to warm.

The beauties of the gardens during this time are often more subtle than in the summer. Under the pall of leaden skies on a cold, damp December day, the crumpled remnants of leaves and the stark outlines of the trees can seem a sorrowful contrast to the times when there are beds glowing with flowers or groves ablaze with autumn color. But it is one of the best times to notice bark patterns, the subtle hues of grasses, the graceful tracery of branches.

Then there are the glorious days of mid-winter when the sky is a brilliant blue and sunshine floods the snow-covered landscape. The gardens become a magical, glittering place where sounds are muffled and the shape of every branch, twig, stone and man-made object is accentuated and softened.

Even before winter draws to a close, the first stirrings of new growth appear. A haze of greening twigs, small patches of new shoots above ground, the brave flowers of witch hazel and hellebore, all announce the coming of spring.

Garden Colors on a Sunny Winter Day. A background of brilliant blue sky and a blanket of sparkling snow heighten the effect of the warm color on the pillars of the sales building and the rosy stems and reddish leaves of rose bushes.

Snow Falling From Cedars.
For a moment, a miniature snowstorm caused by a clump of snow falling from a branch in the distance disrupts the perfect stillness of this winter scene.

Winter In the Children's Garden.
The little pig and Maizie the cow appear to be waiting patiently for warm weather to return, bringing young visitors with it.

Weeping Norway Spruce, *Picea abies* **'Pendula.'** A coat of snow exaggerates the resemblance of this tree to some large prehistoric pachyderm.

Early Winter Afternoon. Rain brings out bold color contrasts on a dull, gray day. Here, red berries of hawthorn, *Crataegus viridis* 'Winter King,' bright green grass, dark mulch, white snow and varying shades of evergreens in the background make a colorful scene despite the weather.

Harbinger of Spring. In late winter the bright yellow flowers of witch hazel, *Hamamelis x intermedia* 'Arnold Promise.' are the first blossoms of the new year in the garden.

Behind the Scenes *Work...* and *Results*

After she draws up her design, the Director of Horticulture and the staff gardeners lay out 30,000 tulip bulbs each fall. The bulbs are then planted by staff and volunteers. During blooming season careful records are kept on the performance of each variety.

Before   After

Before   After

Before   After

It takes approximately 40 hours of skilled work by the Grounds Manager and staff gardeners to prune and train the 27 'Fourth of July' climbers that bloom all summer along the north boundary fence.

All 7,000 roses are cut back, fertilized and mulched with composted leaf mold during March and April. Here the gardeners are mulching the 'Scarlet Meidiland' ground cover roses that provide a brilliant background for the "Boy with the Leaking Boot" statue at the edge of the lake.

SEVENTEEN

Behind the Scenes

The people who keep a public garden in top condition need the same abilities as home gardeners. Knowledge, skill, dedication and muscle power are needed by both groups, as the tasks required are identical. The difference is simply a matter of scale.

Two senior staff plus five full-time and four seasonal gardeners and 45 volunteers work to keep Hershey Gardens looking its best. The Director of Horticulture directs and coordinates all of the horticultural functions of the gardens from the design and ordering of the plant materials for each year's seasonal displays to maintaining plant identification, planning and budgeting.

The gardeners work together as a team, led by the Grounds Manager who also does the spraying, orders equipment and supplies and is the rose expert. Each of the other five full-time gardeners also has a specialty.

Routines vary with the season. Winter chores include pruning, equipment overhaul, non-plant maintenance and snow removal. Spring means general clean-up, taking down the winter deer fencing, cutting back the roses and usually replacing about 250, plus planting annuals and perennials. There is also the start of the edging, weeding, dead-heading, spraying, trimming, mowing and fertilizing which, along with watering, continue all summer. Fall brings another general cleanup, cutting back perennials and roses, planting tulips and other bulbs, draining and cleaning of ponds and putting up the deer fencing.

Although the work is demanding, watching the gardens thrive makes it satisfying. To hear admiring visitor comments and be able to answer their questions is also a pleasure. That, the gardeners say, "is the fun part."

Keeping the gardens in good shape is labor intensive.

Watering. Even under the best conditions some watering is needed on a regular basis. The main parts of the gardens have irrigation systems, but others do not and are watered by hose or watering cans supplied from the 200 gallon mobile tank in this photograph.

Mowing. One day a week, seven gardeners put in a total of 42 hours of mowing in order to keep the lawns approximately three inches high. Beds are trimmed the day before. Lawns are edged, as needed, on a continuing basis.

Dead-heading Annuals. Another weekly job throughout the summer months, both annuals and perennials must have dead flowers and leaves removed in order to look their best.

Dead-heading Roses. Once a week, gardeners and volunteers cut out the dead roses on the climbers and in the rose beds.

Cutting Back Perennials. A job for early fall, each plant must be cut back according to its particular needs.

Planting. Spring and fall are the main planting seasons. In this photograph the plants for the new Bowman Garden are being planted in the fall of 2005.

Putting up Deer Fence. Each fall, deer fence must be put up to protect the vegetation. Here, posts and mesh fencing are being installed around the rock garden. Mesh is also used to cover the year-round main garden fence and extend its height during the winter months.

Fall Clean Up. A major part of fall clean-up is leaf removal. Leaves and other plant materials are composted on site.

Machinery Maintenance. One gardener has the responsibility of keeping the vitally important garden machinery in working order. This includes routine maintenance throughout the year and complete overhaul during the winter months.

Front Cover: Main picture: *Alan Wycheck Photography, Harrisburg, PA;* inset: *Picture-Perfect Photography by Cisco-Adler, York, PA.* **Page 3:** *Picture Perfect Photography by Cisco Adler, York, PA.*
Pages 4-5: Main picture: *Alan Wycheck Photography, Harrisburg, PA* **Page 5:** Top and bottom-*Peter Houts.*
Pages 6-7: *Peter Houts.* **Pages 8-9:** Main picture: *Michael Seligson;* all others-*Peter Houts.* **Pages 10-11:** Main picture: *Colleen Seace.* **Page 10:** Left-*Peter Houts;* bottom right-*Ann Phillips.* **Page 11:** Bottom-*Colleen Seace.*
Pages 12-13: Main pictures: Top-*Everlasting Images Photography; Hershey, PA;* bottom-*Richard Williams.* **Page 12:** Bottom left-*Hershey Community Archives.* **Page 13:** Right side-*Peter Houts.* **Pages 14-15:** Left-*Mary Houts;* all others-*Peter Houts.* **Page 16:** *Peter Houts.* **Page 17:** *Picture Perfect Photography by Cisco-Adler, York, PA.* **Pages 18-19:** *Hershey Community Archives.* **Pages 20-21:** Hershey Park Entrance, ca.1920-29; Hershey Park, ca. 1915 and Harry Haverstick, Hershey's First Chief Gardener, 1917-*Neil Fasnacht Collection;* all others-*Hershey Community Archives.* **Pages 22-23:** *Hershey Community Archives.*
Pages 24-25: J. Horace McFarland, Environmentalist and Rose Expert 1947-*Pennsylvania State Archives;* View Looking North from the Reflecting Pond, Summer, 1938 - *Curt Teich Postcard Archives, Lake County Discovery Museum, Wauconda,IL;* World War II Soldier at Hershey Rose Garden, Early 1940's-*Ellis Kreider;* all others-*Hershey Community Archives.* **Pages 26-27:** *Peter Houts.* **Pages 28-29:** Tulip time – Tulips-*W. Allen Boyer,* Costumed employee-*Judy White;* Easter Sunrise Service-*Carol Humphreys;* Leone Gerberich Pruning-*Hershey Gardens;* all others-*Hershey Community Archives.* **Pages 30-31:** *Hershey Gardens.* **Pages 32-33:** Tulips in Hershey Gardens, 1987 and Hershey Gardens Roses, 1987-*Leone Gerberich;* all others-*Hershey Community Archives.* **Pages 34-35:** *Peter Houts.* **Pages 36-37:** Barbara Whitcraft, Director of Horticulture, 2005-*George Weigel;* "Cool Color" Annuals, Restored Rose Garden- *Picture Perfect Photography by Cisco Adler, York, PA;* Tai Chi Class-*Colleen Seace;* Education Building, 2003-*Crystal Huff;* Deer's Eye View of tulip Beds-*Mary Houts;* Butterfly House, Exterior and Interior-*Richard Williams;* Bill Bowman Garden, Fall, 2005-*Michael Seligson;* all others-*Barbara Whitcraft.* **Pages 38-39:** Views Towards Hotel Hershey, 1938, 1951, *Curt Teich Postcard Archives, Lake County Discovery Museum, Wauconda, IL;* 2005-*Peter Houts.* **Pages 40-41** Gazebo Under Construction-*Marlin Buck;* Boy With Leaking Boot ca. 1960-*Neil Fashnacht Collection,* Boy With Boot, 2005-*Michael Seligson;* Rebecca at the Well, 2005-*Janet Maynard;* Northeast View of Rebecca Statue, 1940- *Curt Teich Postcard Archives, Lake County Discovery Museum, Wauconda,IL;* Sales Building ca. 1948 and Rose Garden Beds, 1937-*Hershey Community Archives;* all others-*Peter Houts.* **Page 42:** Hershey Gardens Map-*Russ Cox/Smiling Otis Studio. Lancaster, PA.* **Page 43:** *Picture Perfect Photography by Cisco Adler, York, PA.* **Pages 44-47:** *Peter Houts.* **Pages 48-49:** *Michael Seligson.* **Pages 50-51:** First Bulbs of the Season-*Mary Houts;* On a Perfect Spring Day, Mid-Spring-*Michael Seligson;* all others-*Peter Houts.* **Pages 52-53:** *Peter Houts.* **Pages 54-55:** On a Mid-Spring Afternoon-*Colleen Seace;* all others-*Peter Houts.* **Pages 56-61:** *Peter Houts.* **Pages 62-63:** Weeping Beech Gateway, Herb Garden-*Mary Houts;* Mrs. Hershey's Rose Garden-*Picture Perfect Photography by Cisco Adler,York, PA;* all others-*Peter Houts.* **Pages 64-71:** *Peter Houts.* **Pages 72-73:** Children's Garden Map-*Russ Cox/Smiling Otis Studio, Lancaster, PA.* **Pages 74-75:** Say Hello to A Friendly Bee, Make Up Stories, Grind Corn , Listen to a story, Enjoy the misty spray , Dance on the Dance Chimes, Climb a Pig-*Colleen Seace;* Sail in a Boat-*Ann Phillips;* all others-*Peter Houts.* **Pages 76-77:** Main picture-*Peter Houts;* Butterflies: (L. to R.)1& 2-*Colleen Seace;* 3-5-*Richard A. Walter;* 6-*Richard Williams.* **Pages 78-79:** Butterflies Visiting Visitors (l)-*Colleen Seace;* (r)-*Donna Bresaw;* Replenishing the House, Caterpillars Explained-*Richard Williams;* Caterpillar Boxes-*Michael Seligson;* Chrysalids-*Janet Maynard;* All others-*Mary Houts.* **Pages 80-81:** *Janet Maynard.* **Pages 82-83:** Snow Falling from Cedars, Winter Color-*Mary Houts;* all others-*Peter Houts.* **Pages 84-85:** Bottom Right-*Michael Seligson;* all others-*Peter Houts.* **Page 86:** Dead-heading roses, Planting, Deer fence, Fall clean up- *Peter Houts;* all others-*Mary Houts.* **End Page:** *Peter Houts.* **Back Cover:** History-*Hershey Community Archives;* all others-*Peter Houts.*